Explore the Universe
GALAXIES

WORLD BOOK

a Scott Fetzer company
Chicago
www.worldbookonline.com

World Book, Inc.
233 N. Michigan Avenue
Chicago, IL 60601
U.S.A.

For information about other World Book publications, visit our Web site at **http://www.worldbookonline.com** or call **1-800-WORLDBK (967-5325).**

For information about sales to schools and libraries, call **1-800-975-3250 (United States),** or **1-800-837-5365 (Canada).**

Library of Congress Cataloging-in-Publication data
Galaxies.
   p. cm. -- (Explore the universe)
  Summary: "An introduction to galaxies with information about their formation and characteristics. Includes diagrams, fun facts,
glossary, resource list, and index"--Provided by publisher.
  Includes index.
  ISBN 978-0-7166-9549-3
  1. Galaxies--Juvenile literature. I. World Book, Inc.
  QB857.3.G345 2010
  523.1'12--dc22

          2009042584

ISBN 978-0-7166-9544-8 (set)
Printed in China by Leo Paper Products LTD.,
  Heshan, Guangdong
1st printing February 2010

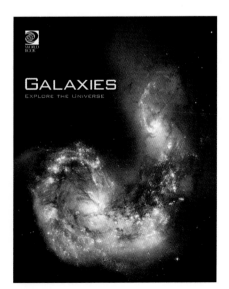

Cover image:
Streaming clusters of bright, massive stars (colorized in blue) and clouds of hydrogen gas (pink) illuminate the colliding Antennae Galaxies. The two spiral galaxies began merging from 200 million to 300 million years ago. Nearly all of the new star clusters in the galaxies are expected to burn out within only 10 million years.

NASA, ESA, and The Hubble Heritage Team (STScI/AURA)-ESA/Hubble Collaboration

CONTENTS

Introduction 4

What is a galaxy? 6

How many galaxies are there? 8

FOCUS ON: Grouping Galaxies 10

What is a spiral galaxy? 12

What is an elliptical galaxy? 14

What is an irregular galaxy? 16

FOCUS ON: Peculiar Galaxies 18

Do galaxies usually exist in groups? 20

How large are galaxies? 22

Which is the most distant galaxy? 24

FOCUS ON: The Galaxy We Live In 26

What is the nearest galaxy to ours? 28

Do galaxies move around? 30

How fast does a galaxy move? 32

Do galaxies ever merge? 34

FOCUS ON: Colossal Collisions 36

Who discovered that galaxies exist? 38

Why does a galaxy glow? 40

How do astronomers use light to study galaxies? 42

How do astronomers count galaxies? .44

When did galaxies start to form? 46

How did galaxies form? 48

Are new stars forming in galaxies? 50

Are galaxies forming now? 52

FOCUS ON: Gravity—A Galactic Glue 54

Can galaxies die? 56

What are some remaining mysteries about galaxies? 58

Glossary 60

For more information 62

Index 63

Acknowledgments 64

If a word is printed in **bold letters that look like this,** that word's meaning is given in the glossary on pages 60-61.

INTRODUCTION

At night, the Milky Way stretches like a white band across the sky. Ancient people described it as a river of spilled milk. Today we know that the Milky Way is actually a galaxy, a vast system of stars, gas, dust, and other matter. As massive as it seems, however, our home galaxy is only one of billions, perhaps trillions, of galaxies in the universe.

Some of these other galaxies are relatively close to the Milky Way. In fact, the Milky Way is consuming some of its nearest neighbors, and it may collide with another large galaxy within a few billion years. Other galaxies are incredibly far away. Light from the most distant galaxies observed so far traveled for more than 13 billion years to reach us. Such light left its home when the universe was young.

Great arms of dust, gas, and stars sweep from the bright core of M74, a spiral galaxy thought to resemble the Milky Way. M74 is one of a small number of galaxies that can be seen nearly "face on" from Earth.

STARS, DUST, AND GAS

Galaxies resemble islands of **stars** in the vast emptiness of space. Most galaxies contain billions of stars. A star is a gigantic glowing ball of gas and **plasma** held together by its own **gravity.** The sun is a star.

In addition to stars, galaxies have vast amounts of dust and gas. Astronomers call the dust and gas between stars the **interstellar medium.** A thick cloud of this matter is called a **nebula.** Most of the material in the interstellar medium is made of such light **chemical elements** as **hydrogen** and **helium.** There may also be smaller amounts of heavier elements, such as oxygen and iron.

MANY TYPES AND SIZES

Galaxies come in all sizes and types. There are galaxies with fewer than 100,000 stars and some that may contain several trillion. **Spiral galaxies** look like pinwheels. **Elliptical galaxies** look like ovals. **Irregular galaxies** come in a variety of shapes.

Vast clouds of dust and gas hide the light of stars in the spiral galaxy NGC 5866, whose edge faces Earth. Star clusters composed of nearly 1 million stars each pepper the galaxy's transparent outer halo.

DID YOU KNOW?

Some astronomers estimate that as many as one-third of the stars in all known galaxies have planets orbiting them.

A galaxy is a huge grouping of stars, dust, gas, and other matter held together by their mutual gravitational pull.

The Black Eye Galaxy, known formally as M64, gets its name from the dark clouds of dust along the edge visible from Earth. The galaxy consists of two systems of stars that rotate in opposite directions, probably the result of a merger of two individual galaxies.

Using a supercomputer, astronomers in Europe estimated that there could be as many as 500 billion **galaxies** in the *observable universe* (the part of the universe that we can see). Some astronomers believe there are trillions of galaxies in the observable universe.

UNSEEN GALAXIES

Some galaxies are so far away that they cannot be seen in the **visible light** that **optical** telescopes collect. Light from these galaxies reaches Earth as **radio waves** or **infrared light,** which are forms of **electromagnetic radiation** with **wavelengths** longer than those of visible light. Astronomers use special telescopes to observe these galaxies.

As astronomers develop more-powerful telescopes, our view of the universe expands. However, some galaxies are so far away that the expansion of the universe has carried them beyond our view forever. As a result, we will probably never be able to say for certain how many galaxies exist in the universe.

The 1.6 million galaxies that appear in a false-color image of the universe represent only a fraction of all galaxies. The dimmest, most distant galaxies are shown in red, while the nearest, brightest galaxies appear in blue. The map was based on data from the Two-Micron Sky Survey.

Galaxies come in an amazing variety of sizes and shapes, as shown in this collection of 196 of the 100 million nearby galaxies surveyed in ultraviolet light by the Galaxy Evolution Explorer probe. The images are arranged to show how galaxies change as they age. Younger galaxies (blue) are forming many new stars. Galaxies with a soft, golden glow contain many older stars.

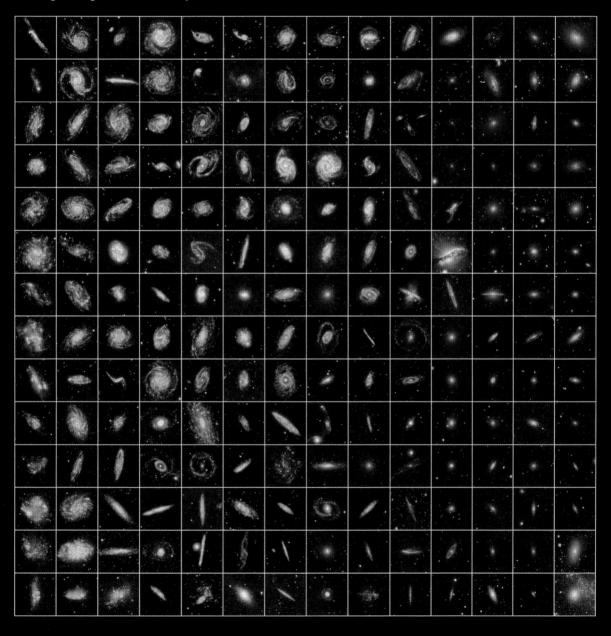

FOCUS ON

GROUPING GALAXIES

THE HUBBLE TUNING FORK

American astronomer Edwin P. Hubble was the first scientist to classify galaxies based on their shape. Astronomers still use his system, which is called the Hubble tuning fork.

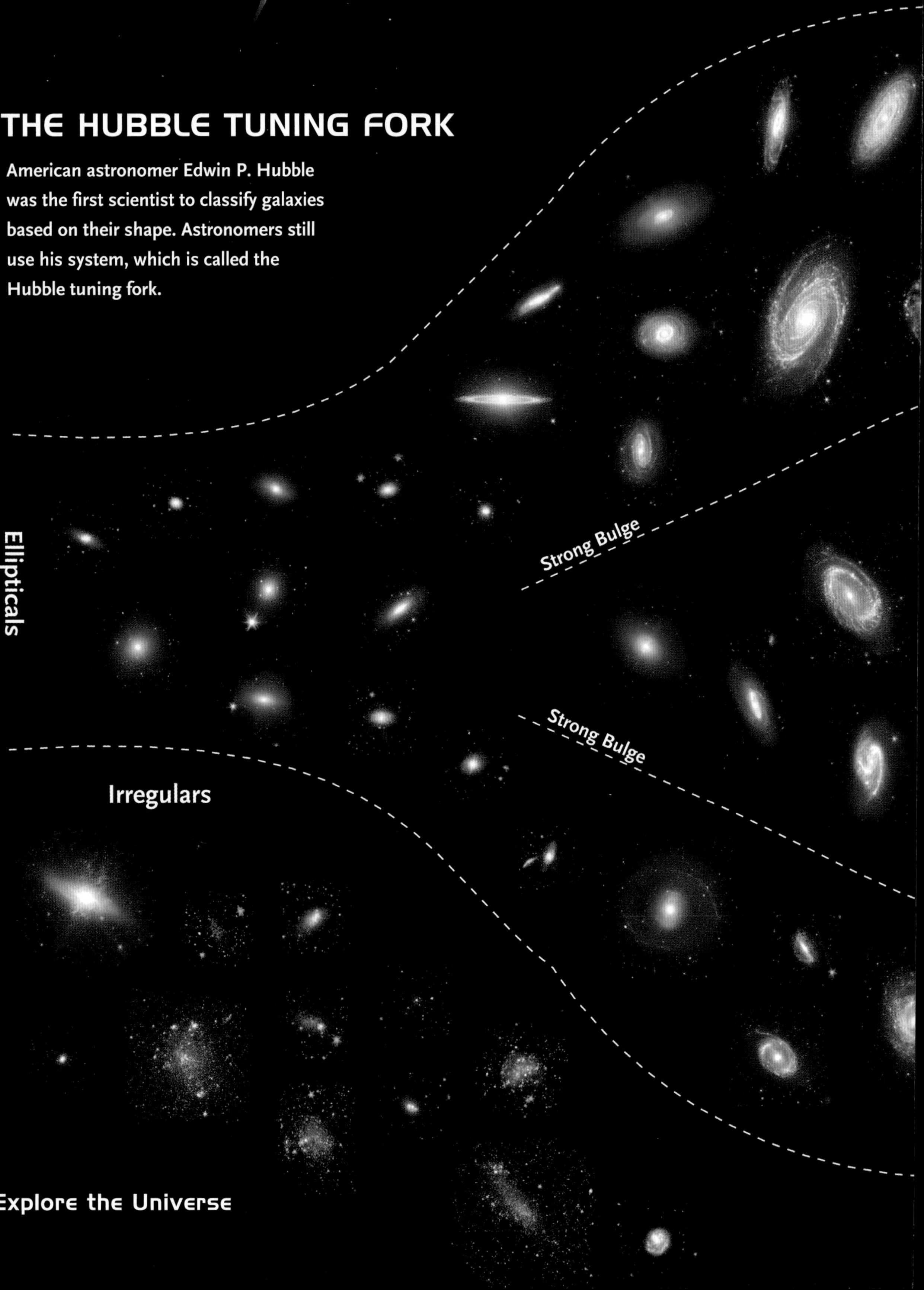
Ellipticals
Strong Bulge
Strong Bulge
Irregulars

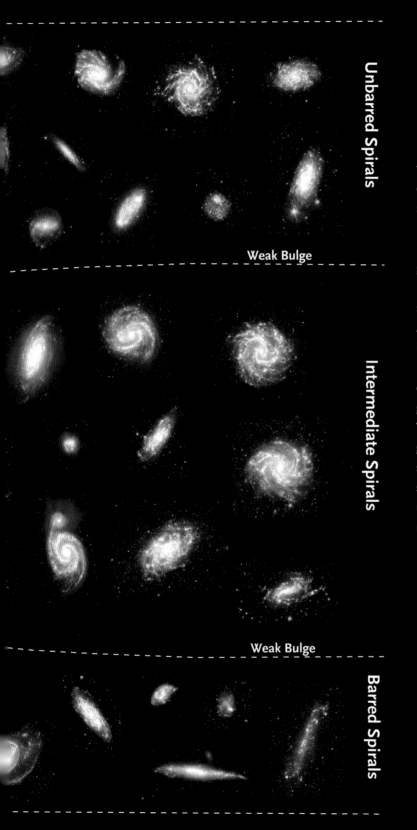

Weak Bulge

Weak Bulge

Hubble divided galaxies into two basic types: elliptical and spiral galaxies. An elliptical galaxy is oval in shape, and a spiral galaxy is shaped like a pinwheel.

Elliptical galaxies are classified by how round or flat they look. Spiral galaxies are classified by whether they have a central bar. Galaxies with this structure are called barred spiral galaxies. A spiral is also classified by how tightly its arms wrap around its center.

Some galaxies show features of both elliptical and spiral galaxies. Other galaxies do not show features of either. These galaxies are called irregular galaxies. They come in any number of shapes. These galaxies are often quite small, and many have been pulled into unusual shapes by the gravity of nearby neighbors.

DISK AND SPIRAL ARMS

From the side, **spiral galaxies** resemble Frisbees. When viewed from the top, they resemble pinwheels. Sweeping arms of **stars** wrap around the center of a **galaxy**. The arms of spiral galaxies appear so bright because they contain many hot stars with great **mass** (amount of matter). Such stars give off far more light than stars with less mass, such as the sun. These huge stars shine for only millions of years, compared with the sun's expected lifetime of 10 billion years. **Nebulae** of dust and gas also glow within the spiral arms, illuminated by the stars nearby. New stars form from this material.

The spaces between the bright arms of a spiral galaxy have more matter than they appear to. As the disk rotates, **gravity** causes stars to pile up along spiral waves within the disk. These waves also allow clouds of dust and gas to pile up in the same spiral pattern. Massive stars are usually born in such areas. As these short-lived stars die off, only the dimmer, lower-mass stars remain. That portion of the disk fades as the wave passes to a new part of the disk, repeating the process. The regions between the arms contain mostly older, dimmer stars that give off relatively little **visible light** and so appear dark.

NGC 1097 shows the pinwheel shape typical of spiral galaxies. Spiral arms trail from a long central bar. A bright ring of newborn stars is visible in the galaxy's core.

CENTRAL BULGE AND BAR

At the center of a spiral galaxy, a bulge of stars, dust, and gas extends above and below the disk. In many large galaxies, the stars in the center form a bar. The spiral arms extend out from the ends of the bar. Galaxies like the Milky Way with a central bar are called barred spiral galaxies.

Seen from the top, a spiral galaxy resembles an enormous pinwheel. The arms of the galaxy spiral around its center.

The spiral Sombrero Galaxy, whose edge faces Earth, appears as a thin disk of dust surrounding a brilliant core. The galaxy is 50,000 light-years across, about half the diameter of the Milky Way.

The spiral arms of the Whirlpool Galaxy (left) may owe their unusual appearance to streams of stars and dust pulled from a smaller nearby galaxy (above).

NGC 1316 is a bright elliptical galaxy that astronomers believe formed several billion years ago when two spiral galaxies collided.

Elliptical galaxies are oval in shape. They may be long like an egg, round like a globe, or slightly flattened.

ENDLESS VARIETY

Elliptical galaxies come in a variety of shapes. Some are nearly round, and others appear flattened. An elliptical's shape is determined by the orbits of individual **stars** in it. The stars in round elliptical galaxies have randomly tilted orbits. Stars in flattened elliptical galaxies tend to have orbits closer to the same plane and do not form the disks found in **spiral galaxies.** Ellipticals also vary greatly in size and brightness. They include some of the largest and smallest as well as the brightest and dimmest known galaxies. The center of an elliptical is the brightest part, with the brightness fading toward the edges.

OLDER STARS

Most ellipticals are thought to be made up of older stars that are billions of years old. These ellipticals contain little gas. Because new stars form from such gas, relatively few new stars form in most elliptical galaxies.

A massive, glowing halo of hot gas giving off X rays surrounds galaxy NGC 1132, one of the largest known galaxies, in a false-color image taken by the Hubble Space Telescoope. NGC 1132 is probably a "fossil galaxy"—the remains of a number of galaxies that were devoured by a large "cannibal galaxy."

WHAT IS AN IRREGULAR GALAXY?

M82, also known as the Cigar Galaxy, is a starburst galaxy that has been pulled into an irregular shape by the gravity of a large, nearby spiral galaxy.

DID YOU KNOW?

A starburst galaxy is a galaxy where stars are forming at a rate hundreds of thousands of times as great as that in the Milky Way.

Irregular galaxies typically have a patchy, disorderly appearance. They do not qualify as either spiral or elliptical.

COSMIC ODD BALLS

Irregular galaxies come in a variety of shapes. In most irregular galaxies, **star** formation occurs in separate regions, giving them a patchy, disorderly appearance. Most irregular galaxies have much lower **mass** (amount of matter) than a large galaxy such as the Milky Way.

AMPLE DUST AND GAS

Compared with **spiral** or **elliptical galaxies,** irregular galaxies typically contain more of their visible matter in the form of dust and gas than in stars. Irregular galaxies contain enough material to form stars for billions of years into the future.

HOW THEY FORMED

Astronomers think irregular galaxies may form in different ways. Many irregular galaxies have been pulled out of a regular shape by the **gravity** of another galaxy. Other irregulars have too little mass to form the density waves that generate spiral arms.

Massive clusters of brilliant new stars light up the irregular dwarf galaxy NGC 1569 in a false-color image taken by the Hubble Space Telescope. Astronomers estimate that the intense star formation began in NGC 1569 only about 25 million years ago.

FOCUS ON

PECULIAR GALAXIES

Peculiar galaxies feature unusual shapes. These systems may result from such dramatic events as the collision of two or more galaxies.

A ring of massive, brilliant, newly formed stars surrounds the Cartwheel Galaxy, shown in a false-color composite image from four space telescopes. Astronomers believe the ring was created when one of the smaller galaxies shown at left in the image passed through the larger galaxy. The collision sent a shock wave through the Cartwheel Galaxy that set off a burst of star formation in its core. The wave of star formation has moved outward from the collision point over time, creating what astronomers call a ring galaxy. ▼

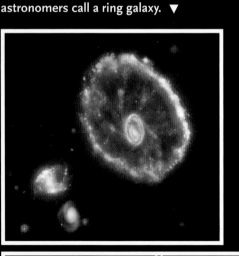

Different wavelengths of light show different gases and materials as different temperatures. ▼

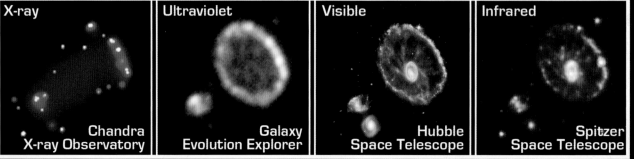

X-ray	Ultraviolet	Visible	Infrared
Chandra X-ray Observatory	Galaxy Evolution Explorer	Hubble Space Telescope	Spitzer Space Telescope

A "tail" of stars and gas more than 280,000 light-years long streams behind the Tadpole Galaxy because of a collision with a much smaller galaxy (arrow). The collision produced strong gravitational forces that pulled long strings of stars and other matter away from the Tadpole Galaxy. The intruder galaxy now appears to be moving away from the Tadpole Galaxy.

Like the Cartwheel Galaxy, Galaxy AM 0644-741 (background image) formed a ring of stars when a smaller galaxy passed through it, much like a stone thrown into a pond creates a circular ripple. Astronomers believe these so-called ring galaxies are created when a large spiral galaxy and a smaller companion galaxy crash into each other nearly head-on.

GROUPS AND CLUSTERS

Few **galaxies** are isolated in space. Most are members of either **groups** or **clusters.** Groups contain 20 to 100 galaxies. The Milky Way belongs to a system called the Local Group. This group occupies an area about 10 million **light-years** across. A light-year is the distance light travels in one year, which is equal to about 5.88 trillion miles (9.46 trillion kilometers). The Local Group contains some 40 galaxies, including two **irregular galaxies** near the Milky Way, the Large and Small Magellanic Clouds. It also contains another large **spiral galaxy** similar to the Milky Way, called the Andromeda Galaxy. The smaller galaxies in the Local Group orbit around the larger Milky Way and Andromeda galaxies.

Clusters contain more galaxies than groups do. The cluster nearest to our galaxy is the Virgo Cluster, about 55 million light-years away. It contains about 2,500 galaxies, including a number of large **elliptical galaxies** at its center.

SUPERCLUSTERS AND WALLS

Groups and clusters belong to **superclusters.** The Local Group belongs to the Local Supercluster, also called the Virgo Supercluster. The Local Supercluster is about 200 million light-years across. It contains tens of thousands of galaxies. Neighboring superclusters are between 100 million and 300 million light-years away.

Astronomers studying the large-scale structure of the universe have found that superclusters make up huge **galactic walls.** One of the largest of these structures, called the Great Wall, is about 600 million light-years long. These structures are separated by **galactic voids,** areas that contain no galaxies. The largest void discovered so far is about 1 billion light-years across.

The sun actually has relatively few close neighbors. The nearest star, Proxima Centauri, is 4.2 light-years away. This distance is slightly less than the average distance between the stars in our section of the Milky Way. Stars in the galactic center are about 100 times as close together. Only one large galaxy, Andromeda, lies within 500,000 light-years of the Milky Way. However, at least 12 smaller galaxies orbit within this distance.

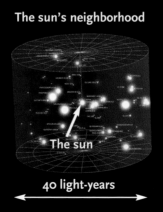

The sun's neighborhood

The sun

40 light-years

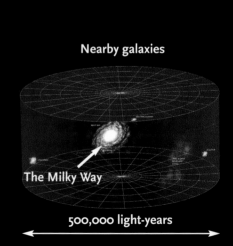

Nearby galaxies

The Milky Way

500,000 light-years

Almost all galaxies are part of a collection of galaxies. There are groups, clusters, and superclusters, all held together by the force of gravity.

901a

Abell 901b

902

SW Group

The galaxies that make up the supercluster Abell 901/902 (left, center image) have formed in areas with concentrations of a mysterious form of matter called dark matter (shaded pink), as shown in a composite image. Astronomers believe that dark matter acts as a framework that attracts visible matter, shaping the structure of the universe. The image was created by combining an image of the supercluster taken in visible light with a map of its dark matter.

The Milky Way is part of the Local Group, a concentration of about 40 galaxies that occupy a roughly spherical region of space around 10 million light-years in diameter. The Local Group is part of the Local Supercluster, which has a diameter of about 150 million light-years.

Local Supercluster

The Local Group

Local Group

The Milky Way

10 million light-years

150 million light-years

MONSTER ELLIPTICALS

Huge **elliptical galaxies** exist in the center of big **clusters.** Astronomers believe these **galaxies** grow by drawing in all the smaller galaxies near them. The largest known galaxy might contain 100 trillion **stars** and be about 6 million **light-years** wide. By comparison, the Milky Way is about 100,000 light-years wide. One elliptical, called IC 1101, is in a cluster of thousands of galaxies named Abell 2029, about 1 billion light-years from Earth. The galaxy likely grew to such a large size by consuming other galaxies in the cluster.

MESSIER 87

The largest galaxy in our galactic neighborhood is a giant elliptical called M87, which is about 60 million light-years from Earth. It is located at the center of the Virgo Cluster. M87 is about 120,000 light-years across, which is not much wider than the Milky Way. However, M87 is shaped like a ball, and the Milky Way is shaped like a disk. As a consequence, M87 has a much larger volume that contains much more **mass** (amount of matter). It contains trillions of stars.

GALACTIC PIPSQUEAKS

At the other extreme, certain **dwarf galaxies** are only about 10,000 light-years across. They contain as few as 100,000 stars. Certain **irregular galaxies** are the smallest of all. Astronomers have found irregular galaxies as small as 1,000 light-years across.

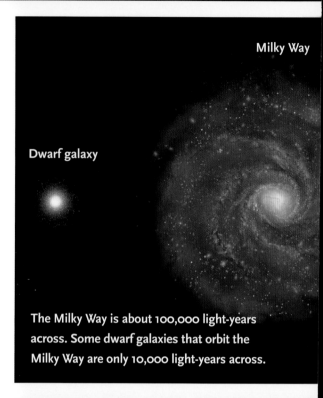

Dwarf galaxy

Milky Way

The Milky Way is about 100,000 light-years across. Some dwarf galaxies that orbit the Milky Way are only 10,000 light-years across.

The elliptical galaxy IC 1101 (above, center) is believed to be the largest known galaxy. IC 1101 has a diameter about 60 times as large as the Milky Way's and contains an estimated 100 trillion stars.

The largest galaxies discovered so far are giant elliptical galaxies about 6 million light-years across. The smallest galaxies are only 1,000 light-years across.

The Sagittarius Dwarf Irregular Galaxy is only about 10,000 light-years across, or about 1/10 as wide as the disk of the Milky Way. The smallest dwarf galaxies may be only 1/100 as wide as the Milky Way.

The galactic cluster Abell 1689 (yellow galaxies in foreground) bends space with its gravity, acting as a lens that magnifies galaxies in the distance. The curving, smeared shapes around the cluster are galaxies behind it. Light from one of these galaxies (right) traveled 13 billion light-years to reach Earth.

DAWN IN THE DISTANCE

Although light moves faster than anything else in the universe, it may still travel for billions of years before reaching us. The light from the most distant known **galaxy** began its journey 13 billion years ago, only about 700 million years after the **big bang.** At that time, the universe was only about 5 percent of its current age of 13.7 billion years. When we observe the most distant galaxies, we are also looking back in time, to when both the galaxies and the universe were young.

COSMOLOGICAL REDSHIFT

The universe has been expanding since the big bang. As a result, light from distant galaxies shows strong **redshift,** or a shift toward longer, redder **wavelengths.** Put in simple terms, the light has been stretched by the expansion of space, much as a spring is stretched as its ends are pulled apart. **Visible light** from distant galaxies has been stretched so much that it reaches Earth as **infrared** or **radio waves.** This effect is called cosmological redshift.

People sometimes say that the most distant galaxies are 13 billion **light-years** away from us, but the truth is more complicated. A distant galaxy may have been only about 3 billion light-years away when its light left. Because space has expanded, the light had to cross 13 billion light-years to reach us. While this light traveled to us, the expansion of the universe has taken the galaxy even farther from us— it is now about 30 billion light-years away. In fact, scientists think there are countless galaxies that even the most powerful telescope will never be able to detect. The distance between these galaxies and Earth is so great that not even light can keep pace with the expansion of the universe.

Because of the expansion of the universe, the light from this distant galaxy shows a strong redshift. That is, visible light has been stretched into longer, redder infrared light.

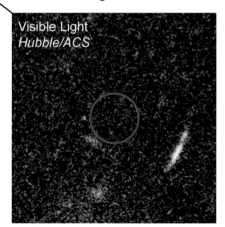

Visible Light
Hubble/ACS

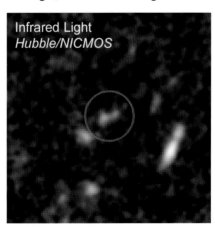

Infrared Light
Hubble/NICMOS

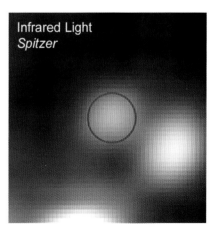

Infrared Light
Spitzer

Our galaxy, the Milky Way, is a barred spiral galaxy about 100,000 light-years across. A vast, thick bar of stars stretches across more than 25,000 light-years of the core. Great spiral arms containing hundreds of billions of stars trail away from either end of the central bar.

Earth, the sun, and the solar system are about 25,000 light-years from the center of the Milky Way. We are about halfway between the center and the outer edge of the galaxy.

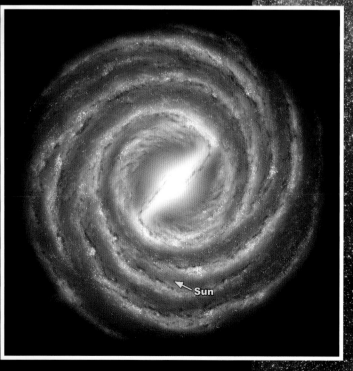

Sun

Far from the light of cities, the Milky Way rises from the horizon like a great river of light. The disk of the Milky Way actually forms a circle that completely surrounds our planet. Clouds of dust and gas hide some of the stars in the disk.

The center of our galaxy is filled with millions of young, bright stars, displayed in an image taken in *infrared* (heat) light by the Spitzer Space Telescope. Infrared light can pass through the great clouds of dust and gas that block *visible light* (light we can see) from the stars.

WHAT IS THE NEAREST GALAXY TO OURS?

DWINDLING DWARFS

The Canis Major Dwarf Galaxy is about 25,000 **light-years** from Earth, which is about the same distance Earth is from the center of the Milky Way. Another **dwarf galaxy,** the Sagittarius Dwarf Elliptical Galaxy, is about 70,000 light-years from Earth. Each of these **galaxies** is much smaller than the Milky Way. In fact, they orbit our galaxy, which is slowly stripping **stars** from them. Eventually, the Milky Way will consume these galaxies entirely.

ANDROMEDA GALAXY

The nearest **spiral galaxy** is the Andromeda Galaxy, about 2.5 million light-years from the Milky Way. Andromeda, which is also known as M31, has an amount of **mass** (amount of matter) similar to that of the Milky Way. However, Andromeda is both brighter and larger, reaching more than 228,000 light-years across. By comparison, the Milky Way is about 100,000 light-years across. Andromeda is one of the most distant objects that can be seen without a telescope.

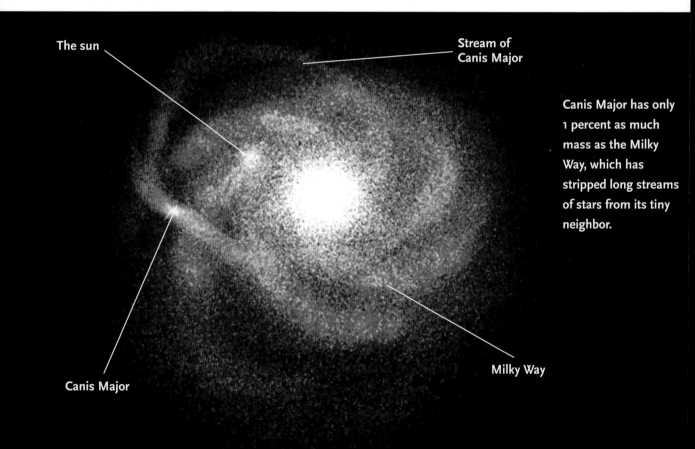

The sun

Stream of Canis Major

Canis Major has only 1 percent as much mass as the Milky Way, which has stripped long streams of stars from its tiny neighbor.

Canis Major

Milky Way

The Andromeda Galaxy is the nearest
spiral galaxy, about 2.5 million light-
years from the Milky Way. It is both
larger and brighter than the Milky
Way, stretching more than 228,000
light-years across.

DO GALAXIES MOVE AROUND?

GALACTIC PIROUETTES

The stars in both **spiral** and **elliptical galaxies** orbit around their galactic cores. For example, the sun completes an orbit inside the Milky Way every 240 million years.

SATELLITES, GROUPS, AND BEYOND

Large galaxies are often surrounded by smaller **satellite galaxies.** In the case of the Milky Way, at least 12 satellite galaxies orbit our large spiral galaxy. Over millions of years, the Milky Way will consume these satellites. The Andromeda Galaxy has more than 14 satellites.

Within **groups** and **clusters,** galaxies orbit around a common center of **gravity.** Within the Local Group that includes our galaxy, the two largest galaxies are the Milky Way and Andromeda. These galaxies are moving toward each other and will likely collide in a few billion years. Groups and clusters themselves move together through space. The Local Group is moving within the Local Supercluster, which contains about 100 groups and clusters. The **supercluster** itself also moves through space.

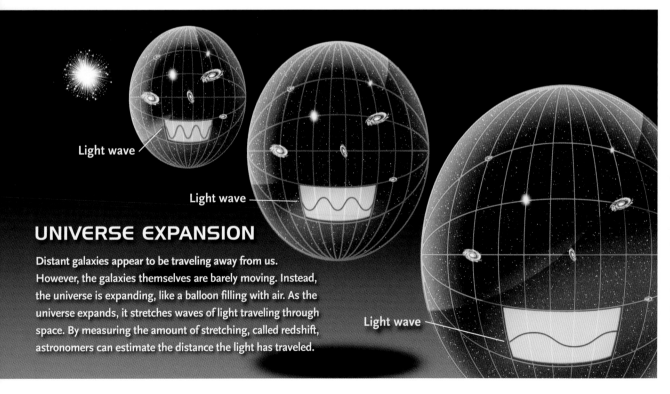

Light wave

Light wave

UNIVERSE EXPANSION

Distant galaxies appear to be traveling away from us. However, the galaxies themselves are barely moving. Instead, the universe is expanding, like a balloon filling with air. As the universe expands, it stretches waves of light traveling through space. By measuring the amount of stretching, called redshift, astronomers can estimate the distance the light has traveled.

Light wave

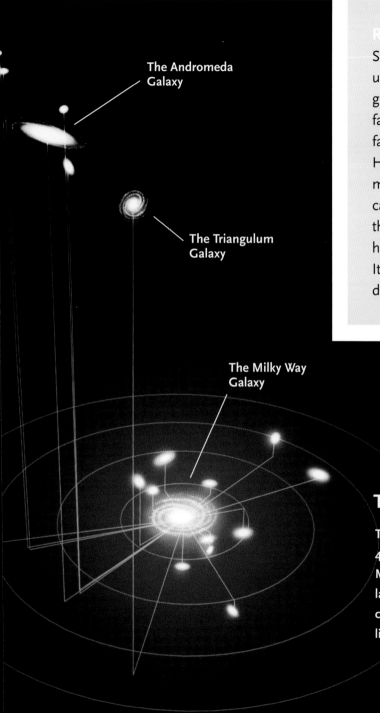

The Andromeda Galaxy

The Triangulum Galaxy

The Milky Way Galaxy

Scientists once thought that the universe was unchanging. Now, we know that distant galaxies are moving away from us. In fact, the farther away one galaxy is from another, the faster those galaxies appear to be moving apart. However, the galaxies themselves are not really moving apart. Rather, their apparent motion is caused by the expansion of space itself. Since the **big bang** 13.7 billion years ago, the universe has grown from a tiny point to its current size. It continues to grow today, increasing the distance between galaxies.

THE LOCAL GROUP

The Local Group consists of about 40 galaxies, most of which orbit the Milky Way and Andromeda, the two largest galaxies. The concentric circles in the diagram are 500,000 light-years apart.

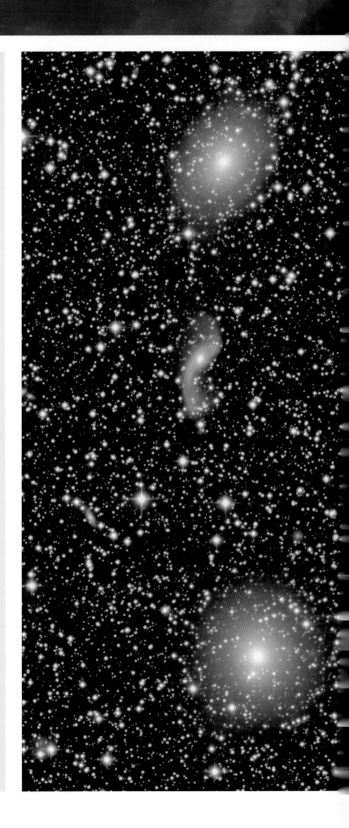

IT'S ALL RELATIVE

There is no center to the universe, so the speed of heavenly objects can only be measured in relation to other objects. For example, the **solar system** is orbiting the center of the Milky Way at 137 miles (220 kilometers) per second. Within the Local Group, Andromeda and the Milky Way are approaching each other at about 75 miles (120 kilometers) per second. **Galaxies** in the Local **Supercluster** move at speeds of more than 930 miles (1,500 kilometers) per second in relation to the supercluster's center. The Local Supercluster itself is rushing through space at about 389 miles (626 kilometers) per second in relation to the **cosmic microwave background (CMB) radiation.** The CMB is the most ancient light in the universe. It is the dim afterglow of the **big bang.**

THE HUBBLE CONSTANT

Distant galaxies also seem to move because the universe has been expanding since the big bang. The rate of this expansion is called the **Hubble constant,** which is equal to about 44 miles (70 kilometers) per second per **megaparsec.** A megaparsec is about 3.26 million **light-years.** The Hubble constant tells us that the more distant two galaxies are, the faster they seem to be moving apart. Galaxies 2 megaparsecs away from each other move apart at 87 miles (140 kilometers) per second. Galaxies 3 megaparsecs away from each other move apart at 130 miles (210 kilometers) per second.

Galaxies move at fantastic speeds. But these speeds can only be measured in relation to other objects.

The Milky Way and all other galaxies within hundreds of millions of light-years are moving toward a great concentration of mass called the Great Attractor. It is difficult to identify the Great Attractor because it is hidden by the disk of our galaxy. It may be an old, extremely massive supercluster that is part of an even larger structure. Our Local Group of galaxies is moving toward the Great Attractor at about 375 miles (600 kilometers) per second.

THE HUBBLE CONSTANT

The Hubble constant is a measure of the rate at which the universe is expanding. Measuring the Hubble constant involves determining the rate at which distant galaxies move away from us and measuring the distance to those galaxies. Astronomers determine this rate by measuring redshift, a stretching of the wavelengths of certain kinds of radiation sent out by celestial objects. By measuring the redshift of light from these galaxies, astronomers can estimate the distance between them and Earth.

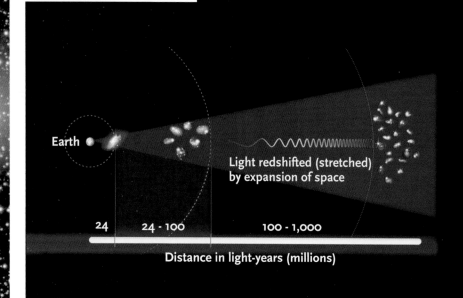

Earth

Light redshifted (stretched) by expansion of space

24   24 - 100   100 - 1,000

Distance in light-years (millions)

DO GALAXIES EVER MERGE?

CANNIBAL GALAXIES

Large **galaxies** often consume nearby **satellite galaxies.** In this way, galaxies may grow in **mass** (amount of matter) over time. Certain **stars** within the Milky Way have unusual orbits that indicate they were stripped from other galaxies in the past. Today, our galaxy is actively stripping stars and other matter from at least 2 of its 12 satellite galaxies.

FROM SPIRAL TO ELLIPTICAL

The pull of **gravity** between galaxies can change their shape. In fact, many **irregular galaxies** were pulled into unusual shapes by the gravity of larger neighbors.

When large **spiral galaxies** merge, they may form an **elliptical galaxy.** Many ellipticals show signs that they were created when spirals merged. The Milky Way and the Andromeda galaxies will likely collide in several billion years. When they do, they may merge to form a new elliptical galaxy.

DID YOU KNOW?

Although galaxies collide, the stars within them rarely do. Stars are small compared with galaxies, so they fly past each other like clouds of gnats. Galactic collisions cause bursts of star formation, as clouds of dust and gas collapse into stars.

Two spiral galaxies known as "The Mice" are captured in the act of merging by the Hubble Space Telescope. The galaxies have already passed through each other once. Clusters of young, massive stars in the galaxy on the left (colorized in bright blue) have formed because of gravitational interactions between the two galaxies.

Astronomers believe that galaxies often merge. As galaxies draw near one another, gravity pulls stars and other matter into streams between them. Eventually, the galaxies may collide and merge.

"Tails" packed with star clusters trail two galaxies that began merging millions of years ago. These galaxies, known as NGC 3256, still have distinct cores. The supermassive black holes in these cores will one day combine and come to rest at the center of a new elliptical galaxy.

COLOSSAL COLLISIONS

The Antennae Galaxies (right) are two large spiral galaxies that began to collide a few hundred million years ago. Their collision has created tremendous star bursts, as their gravity causes clouds of dust and gas to collapse. These galaxies, which are about 45 million light-years away, are the nearest colliding galaxies to Earth. ▶

Three galaxies have collided to form an ▲ unusual object that astronomers have nicknamed the Bird. Two of the galaxies were massive spirals, and the third was an irregular galaxy. The Bird is more than 1 billion times as bright as the sun and has a diameter of 100,000 light-years, about the same as the Milky Way.

Stephan's Quintet (above) is a compact group of galaxies that are colliding and merging. These spiral galaxies will likely become huge elliptical galaxies. The galaxy colorized in dark blue (lower left in image) is much nearer to us than the others and is not a part of the collision.

Spiral galaxies NGC 2207 (above, left) and IC 2163 are pulling each other apart during the early stages of a collision. The smaller galaxy, which is about the size of the Milky Way, is swinging around the larger galaxy in a counterclockwise direction. The merger will take billions of years.

WHO DISCOVERED THAT GALAXIES EXIST?

STARS AND NEBULAE

In the 1600's, the Italian astronomer Galileo Galilei discovered that the white band of light called the Milky Way is made up of individual **stars.** As telescopes became more powerful, astronomers discovered hazy patches of light, which they called **nebulae.** Some of these nebulae were clouds of dust and gas, and these clouds are still called nebulae today. Others were not clouds at all, but telescopes were not powerful to discover their true nature. For hundreds of years, most astronomers thought the Milky Way was the only **galaxy** in the universe.

THE ANDROMEDA "NEBULA"

In 1923, American astronomer Edwin P. Hubble used one of the most powerful telescopes of that time to study the Andromeda Nebula. He found that this nebula contained stars much like those in the Milky Way, but the stars were much fainter. Hubble concluded that Andromeda was actually a separate galaxy. Some astronomers had previously suggested that some "nebulae" were actually other galaxies, but Hubble proved it. His observations forever changed our view of the universe.

HUBBLE'S LAW

In 1929, Hubble discovered that the farther a galaxy is from the Milky Way, the more rapidly it appears to be moving away from us. This apparent motion came to be known as Hubble's law. The rate of the expansion is called the **Hubble constant.** Scientists later discovered that space has been expanding ever since the formation of the universe in the **big bang.**

Edwin Hubble used the 100-inch (2.5-meter) telescope at the Mt. Wilson Observatory to prove that Andromeda is a galaxy.

In the 1920's, American astronomer Edwin P. Hubble discovered that distant blobs of light were actually other galaxies beyond the Milky Way.

DID YOU KNOW?

The Hubble Space Telescope, launched by the National Aeronautics and Space Administration in 1990, was named in honor of Edwin Hubble.

The Mt. Wilson Observatory once housed the most powerful telescope in the world. Today, light from nearby Los Angeles limits the observations that can be made there.

ATOMIC GLOW

Stars give off **visible light** because the **plasma,** a gas-like substance, of which they are made exists at high temperatures. These high temperatures cause the plasma to glow. In addition to the **visible light** our eyes can see, stars also shine in **infrared, ultraviolet, X rays,** and other forms of **electromagnetic radiation.**

The plasma in a star reaches high temperatures because of **nuclear fusion** reactions in its **core.** In these reactions, *nuclei* (centers) of **hydrogen** *fuse* (join) to create nuclei of **helium.** Nuclei of other **chemical elements** can also fuse, creating elements essential to life such as carbon and oxygen. Nuclear fusion gives off tremendous energy.

THE BIRTH OF STARLIGHT

Stars form when clouds of dust and gas collapse under their own **gravity.** Over millions of years, clumps of dust and gas become dense, spinning balls. As a ball grows in **mass** (amount of matter) and density, the temperature and pressure of its core also grow. When the temperature reaches 1 million Kelvin (1.8 million °F), nuclear fusion begins. A star will shine as long as it has fuel. Galaxies glow with the light of billions of stars, which also illuminate huge **nebulae** of dust and gas. When massive stars run out of fuel, they may explode as brilliant **supernovae,** briefly outshining all the other stars of the galaxy.

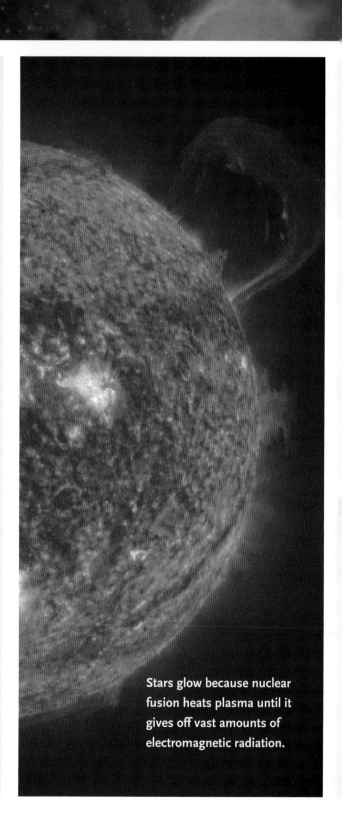

Stars glow because nuclear fusion heats plasma until it gives off vast amounts of electromagnetic radiation.

Galaxies glow with the light of billions of stars.
These stars are powered by nuclear fusion.

Galaxies also glow in forms of light that people cannot see, as revealed in a composite, false-color image of galaxy 3c305 taken by several space and Earth-based telescopes. Visible light from the galaxy appears in light blue, with X rays in red and radio waves in dark blue. The X rays and radio waves are powered by a supermassive black hole in the galaxy's core. Powerful jets from opposite sides of the black hole cause two distant regions to give off radio waves. Matter falling into the black hole gives off tremendous energy, which causes the surrounding gas to give off X rays.

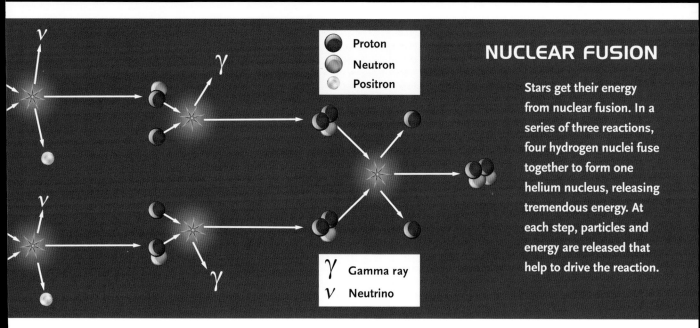

- Proton
- Neutron
- Positron

γ Gamma ray
ν Neutrino

NUCLEAR FUSION

Stars get their energy from nuclear fusion. In a series of three reactions, four hydrogen nuclei fuse together to form one helium nucleus, releasing tremendous energy. At each step, particles and energy are released that help to drive the reaction.

HOW DO ASTRONOMERS USE LIGHT TO STUDY GALAXIES?

FROM BLUE TO RED

The rainbow, or **spectrum,** of light given off by a **star** depends upon its temperature. Young, hot stars shine most brightly in short, blue wavelengths. Old, cool stars shine most brightly in red wavelengths. By analyzing the light given off by **galaxies,** astronomers can calculate the rate at which stars are forming. Young galaxies form stars at a more rapid rate than older galaxies.

ELEMENTAL COLORS

Light also tells astronomers which **chemical elements** are found in the stars of a galaxy. Every element gives off a unique **spectrum.** Stars in galaxies such as the Milky Way contain many heavy elements that were created when stars with high **mass** (amount of matter) exploded as **supernovae.** By contrast, the Small Magellanic Cloud, a neighboring **dwarf galaxy,** has formed relatively few stars. It contains relatively few heavy elements.

Composite images, such as that of the Pinwheel Galaxy (right), combine views from two or more telescopes. They allow scientists to compare various aspects of a heavenly body in one colorized image. Visible light given off by stars in the galaxy, collected by the Hubble Space Telescope, shines brightly in yellow. X-ray emissions from exploded stars, hot gases, and the energy near black holes appear blue in an image from the Chandra X-ray Observatory. Red areas represent heat emissions from dusty areas where stars are forming, collected by the Spitzer Space Telescope.

Doppler shift changes the wavelengths of a galaxy's light depending on its motion. Galaxies moving toward us show blueshift. Galaxies moving away from us show redshift.

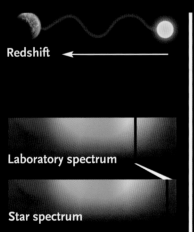

Redshift ←

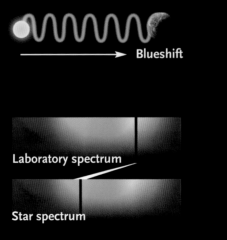

→ Blueshift

Laboratory spectrum

Laboratory spectrum

Star spectrum

Star spectrum

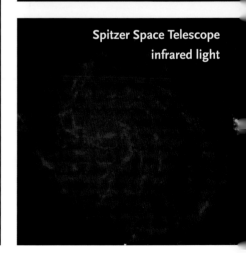

Spitzer Space Telescope infrared light

Astronomers study light from galaxies to learn about temperatures, chemical elements, and the age of a galaxy, as well as how the galaxies are moving through space.

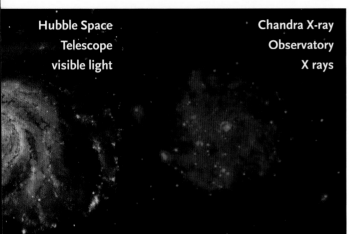

Hubble Space Telescope visible light

Chandra X-ray Observatory X rays

DOPPLER SHIFT

If you have heard a train blow its whistle as it passes, you may have noticed that the whistle sounds higher in pitch as the train approaches and lower as the train speeds away. This shift occurs because the wavelength of the sound is squeezed as the train approaches and stretched as it departs. This shift is called the **Doppler effect,** and it also changes the wavelength of light. Light from nearby galaxies that are approaching us shows **blueshift.** Light from nearby galaxies that are speeding away show **redshift.**

THE EXPANDING UNIVERSE

Distant galaxies all show strong redshift, but it is not caused by the Doppler effect. In fact, it is not caused by the motion of galaxies at all. Instead, distant galaxies show redshift because their light has been stretched by the expansion of the universe. Astronomers call such stretching cosmological redshift, as opposed to Doppler redshift. When astronomers speak of a galaxy's redshift, they are usually referring to its cosmological redshift. By measuring cosmological redshift, astronomers can determine how far the light has traveled. They can then estimate the distance to a galaxy.

HOW DO ASTRONOMERS COUNT GALAXIES?

COUNTING THE BILLIONS

There are billions upon billions of **galaxies.** If you could count one galaxy every second of every day without ever taking a break, you would need more than 30 years to reach a billion.

THE HUBBLE ULTRA DEEP FIELD

To count galaxies, astronomers point their telescopes at small patches of sky for several days. For example, in 2003 and 2004, the Hubble Space Telescope recorded an image called the Hubble Ultra Deep Field. To make this image, the telescope observed a patch of sky so small it is only one-tenth as wide as the moon. In just this one tiny patch of sky, Hubble found more than 10,000 galaxies. Moreover, the image detected only **visible light,** meaning that it missed galaxies that give off only radio waves or other forms of invisible **electromagnetic radiation.**

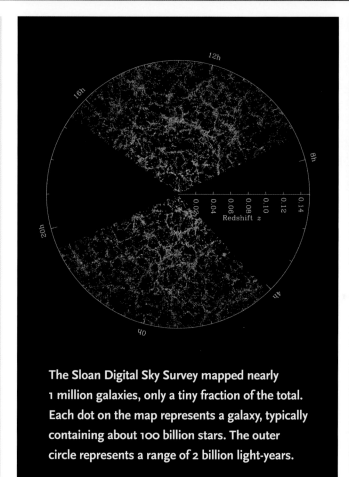

The Sloan Digital Sky Survey mapped nearly 1 million galaxies, only a tiny fraction of the total. Each dot on the map represents a galaxy, typically containing about 100 billion stars. The outer circle represents a range of 2 billion light-years.

OBSERVATIONS AND ESTIMATES

It is not possible to produce deep-field images of the entire sky. Hubble would have to make 13 million separate observations to observe the entire sky in such detail, and this would require more than a million years. Instead, astronomers rely on the assumption that the universe looks much the same in all directions. Based on this conclusion, they can estimate a total. Hubble images indicate that there are 125 billion galaxies in the observable universe. However, the total number of galaxies is certainly much higher.

THE EDGE OF THE INFINITE

More-powerful telescopes currently under construction will be able to detect even dimmer, more distant galaxies. Our tally of galaxies may reach 1 trillion or more.

The Hubble Ultra Deep Field, an image of one section of deep space taken by the Hubble Space Telescope, contains more than 10,000 galaxies. This figure suggests that the observable universe must contain at least 125 billion galaxies.

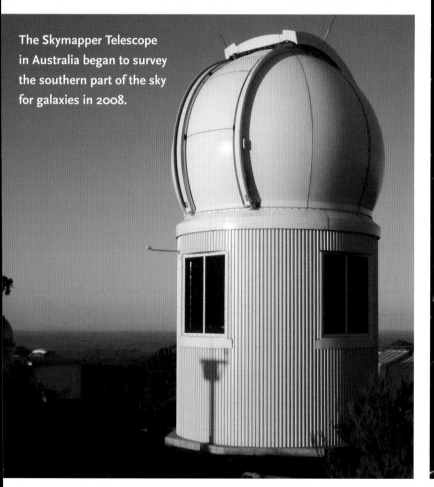

The Skymapper Telescope in Australia began to survey the southern part of the sky for galaxies in 2008.

WHEN DID GALAXIES START TO FORM?

THE DARK AGES

After the **big bang,** the universe was filled with elementary particles and brilliant light. As the universe expanded and cooled, atoms of **hydrogen** formed, which allowed the afterglow of the big bang to travel freely through the universe for the first time. We can still detect this light in the form of the **cosmic microwave background (CMB) radiation.** For many millions of years, the universe was dark, because there were no **stars.** Astronomers call this period the dark ages. They believe that within about 200 million years of the big bang, the first stars formed, ending the dark ages. The first **galaxies** soon followed.

PUSHING THE LIMITS

Astronomers have strong evidence that galaxies formed within 700 million years of the big bang, or about 13 billion years ago. Many scientists, however, believe that galaxies formed even earlier.

In 2007, astronomers using the Keck Observatory found six galaxies that formed within 500 million years of the big bang. The galaxies showed rapid star formation, which astronomers expect from newborn galaxies. Moreover, if six galaxies had already formed within 500 million years of the big bang, their formation must have been underway for many millions of years. However, light from the most distant, ancient galaxies is extremely faint. Astronomers must push their instruments to the very limits in order to learn about the early universe. As a result, much uncertainty and controversy remain about these observations. As scientists build new, more-powerful telescopes, they hope to observe galaxies at the very beginning of their formation.

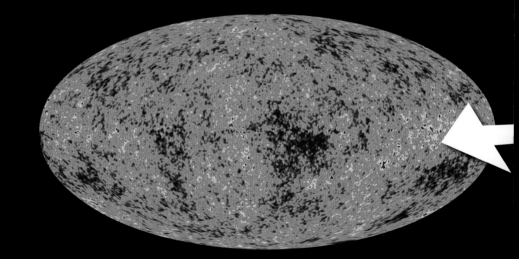

The cosmic microwave background radiation is the most ancient light scientists can detect. This very faint, redshifted light fills the sky in all directions. It was given off millions of years before the first stars and galaxies formed.

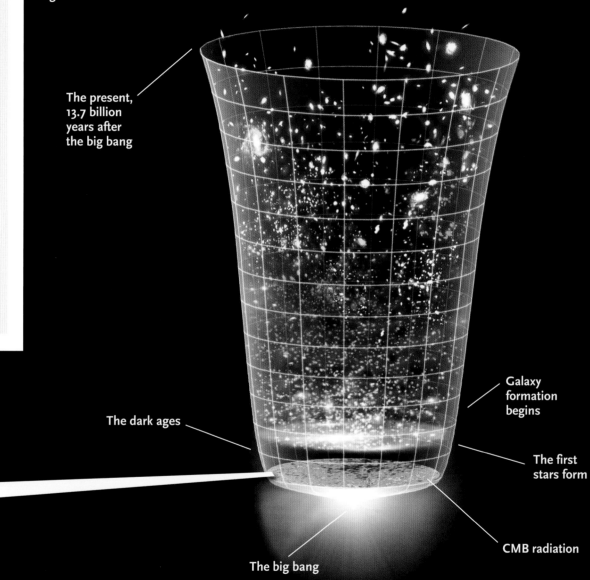

Scientists believe the universe was born in an explosion called the big bang. As the universe cooled, it became dark until the first stars and galaxies formed.

The present, 13.7 billion years after the big bang

The dark ages

The big bang

Galaxy formation begins

The first stars form

CMB radiation

HOW DID GALAXIES FORM?

WITHOUT FORM

As the universe expanded after the **big bang,** it had little structure. There were no **stars** or **galaxies.** In general, matter was spread evenly throughout the universe, though there were some small "lumps." The universe cooled as it expanded, allowing matter to form atoms of **hydrogen.** However, this hydrogen was not concentrated enough to form stars or galaxies.

DARK MATTER

Scientists have found that the matter in stars, **nebulae,** and other bodies makes up only about 15 percent of all matter in the universe. The rest is **dark matter.** Dark matter is a mysterious, invisible form of matter that interacts with ordinary matter only through its gravitational pull. Scientists cannot observe dark matter directly, but they can measure the effects of its **gravity.**

GALACTIC SEEDS

Astronomers believe that pockets of dark matter acted as seeds for the formation of galaxies. The dark matter's gravity pulled in vast amounts of **hydrogen** that formed after the big bang. Eventually, this hydrogen became dense enough to collapse inward and begin to form stars. The large galaxies we observe today formed through repeated collisions and mergers inside clouds of dark matter.

Astronomers have strong evidence that the **superclusters** and **galactic walls** we observe on the largest scales of the universe also formed around concentrations of dark matter. In this way, dark matter shaped the structure of the entire universe. However, we still have much to learn about both dark matter and the crucial role it played in the formation of galaxies.

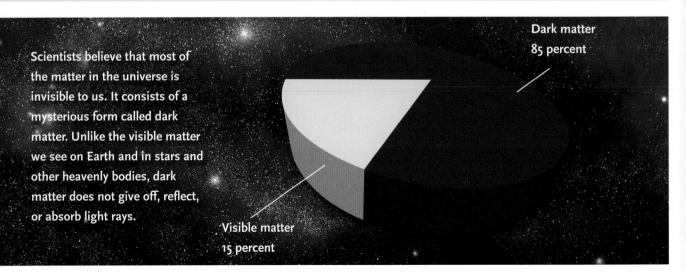

Scientists believe that most of the matter in the universe is invisible to us. It consists of a mysterious form called dark matter. Unlike the visible matter we see on Earth and in stars and other heavenly bodies, dark matter does not give off, reflect, or absorb light rays.

Dark matter
85 percent

Visible matter
15 percent

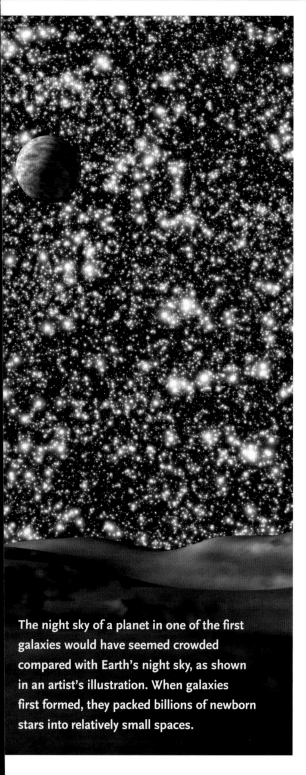

The night sky of a planet in one of the first galaxies would have seemed crowded compared with Earth's night sky, as shown in an artist's illustration. When galaxies first formed, they packed billions of newborn stars into relatively small spaces.

Most astronomers believe that spiral galaxies, like stars, formed from collapsing and rotating clouds of gas and dust.

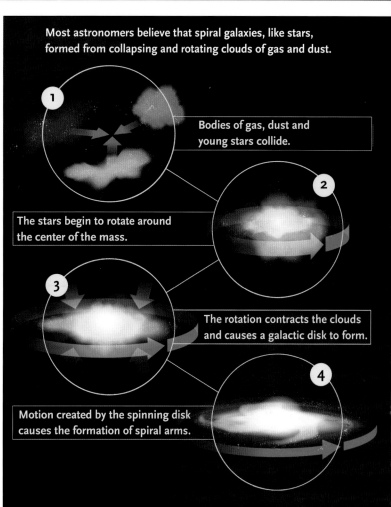

1 Bodies of gas, dust and young stars collide.

The stars begin to rotate around the center of the mass.

2

3 The rotation contracts the clouds and causes a galactic disk to form.

Motion created by the spinning disk causes the formation of spiral arms.

4

DID YOU KNOW?

The halos of dark matter around galaxies could be 10 times as massive as the visible parts of the galaxies. Dark matter is a mysterious form of matter thought to make up the majority of matter in the universe.

ARE NEW STARS FORMING IN GALAXIES?

STARBURSTS

When **spiral galaxies** such as the Milky Way form, they blaze with light as clouds of dust and gas collapse into newborn **stars.** After this burst of intense star formation, the galaxies settle down into a slower rate of star birth. Most new stars form in the core and the spiral arms.

ARRESTED DEVELOPMENT

Irregular and **dwarf galaxies** typically form relatively few stars. These galaxies are too small to form the spiral arms found in larger galaxies, where many stars are born. However, when irregular galaxies draw near larger galaxies, they may give birth to many stars as the **gravity** of their neighbors causes pileups of dust and gas. Many **elliptical galaxies** form relatively few new stars.

Young, blue stars shine from the center of the star-forming region N90 in the Small Magellanic Cloud. Such dwarf galaxies form relatively few new stars.

The spiral galaxy C153 shines with the light of millions of newborn stars in an artist's illustration. Blue trails of gas stream behind the galaxy as it plunges into the heart of a galaxy cluster.

form fewer stars as they age, unless a disturbance causes their remaining clouds of dust and gas to collapse.

Many are thought to have formed when spiral galaxies collided. Ellipticals have consumed much of their dust and gas, and they do not have the arms that give birth to many stars in spiral galaxies.

GALACTIC PILEUPS

Some of the brightest galaxies in the universe are in the midst of colliding with larger neighbors. As two spiral galaxies draw near, the pull of gravity between them compresses dust and gas. Colliding galaxies can form stars at a rate thousands of times as high as usual.

In the Milky Way, stars are born in great clouds of dust and gas in the spiral arms, such as the Orion Nebula.

MERGERS AND ACQUISITIONS

In the young universe, billions of **galaxies** formed from collapsing clouds of gas. In the more mature universe, entirely new galaxies no longer form. However, galaxies often collide or consume their neighbors. When two **spiral galaxies** merge, they may change so greatly that they lose their former identity. In a way, the **elliptical galaxy** that emerges is a new galaxy.

BACK IN TIME

When astronomers observe the distant universe, they are also observing the distant past. Light must travel for billions of years to cross the observable universe. When we observe the light of a galaxy that has traveled 12 billion **light-years,** we see the galaxy as it was 12 billion years ago, not as it is today.

Much of what we know about the development of galaxies has come from studies that use light as a sort of time capsule. For example, astronomers have found thousands of extremely bright objects called **quasars.** They believe these quasars are powered by supermassive **black holes** in the cores of galaxies billions of light-years away. These black holes give off so much light because they are consuming huge amounts of matter. However, astronomers have not found quasars near our galaxy. As a result, they believe that quasars represent a stage many galaxies went through long ago. Today,

A newborn galaxy glows with star formation only 700 million years after the big bang, as shown in an artist's illustration.

Many scientists believe that quasar galaxies such as PKS 1127-145 represent a stage of development many galaxies went through long ago. The supermassive black hole in the core of PKS 1127-145 has produced a powerful jet of material that is visible in this X-ray image.

No entirely new galaxies are forming now. But existing galaxies often change over time, losing their identity through mergers and collisions.

the black holes at the center of most galaxies do not give off intense light, because they are no longer consuming large amounts of matter.

Astronomers have observed relatively small, dim galaxies. These galaxies have not yet grown through repeated collisions and mergers. Astronomers believe these galaxies are in the earliest stages of forming. With more-powerful telescopes, astronomers hope to observe the first galaxies as they formed after the **big bang.**

The unusual galaxy I Zwicky 18 is an old galaxy with many young stars. The presence of so many bright stars in the galaxy led astronomers to conclude that this galaxy was only 500 million years old. The discovery of older, dimmer stars in the galaxy, however, has shown that it is 10 billion years old. Unlike most other galaxies, I Zwicky 18 began forming many new stars later in its life. This intense star formation may have been caused by the gravitational influence of the galaxy's small companion (upper left in image).

GRAVITY—A GALACTIC GLUE

Gravity is the force that rules the universe at large scales, binding matter together into stars and stars together into galaxies. Most matter in the universe is dark matter, an invisible substance that can be detected only through its gravitational pull. Clouds of dark matter acted as seeds for the formation of galaxies. Dark matter also provides the framework for the largest structures in the universe, including superclusters and galactic walls. The gravity of these structures is so powerful that it bends space itself, acting as a giant, invisible lens. This effect is called gravitational lensing.

The gravity of massive objects bends space, acting as a lens that magnifies objects in the distance. This effect can make a galaxy appear as a smeared-out ring of light.

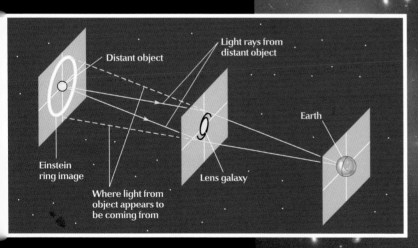

Distant object

Light rays from distant object

Einstein ring image

Where light from object appears to be coming from

Lens galaxy

Earth

GRAVITY RULES THE TITANS

Gravity is the most important force at large scales for objects with a high *mass* (amount of matter). Consider two Earth-sized planets, separated by a distance equal to twice their diameter. Their strong gravitational pull would cause them to smash into each other almost instantly.

Earth-sized planets

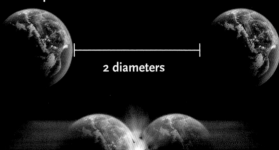

2 diameters

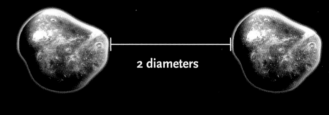

Small asteroids

2 diameters

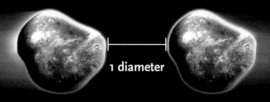

1 diameter

The effects of gravity are not as profound for objects with less mass. Consider two small asteroids, separated by a distance equal to twice their diameter. Gravity would pull the asteroids toward each other but with much less force than in the case of the planets. Even smaller objects, such as two peas, show hardly any gravitational attraction at all.

The cluster CL0024+17 shows a ring of dark matter, illustrated as a bluish, cloudy substance in this Hubble Space Telescope image. Dark matter cannot actually be seen, but its powerful gravity reveals its location. The gravity of the dark matter bends space, causing it to act as a giant, invisible lens. The curving, smeared out galaxies around the cluster (arrows) are actually behind it. Their light has been magnified and distorted by the gravity of the cluster's dark matter.

CAN GALAXIES DIE?

THE DEATH OF BIRTH

As **galaxies** age, they go through repeated collisions and mergers. When galaxies collide, the effects of gravity cause clouds of dust and gas to collapse, forming vast numbers of new **stars.** Eventually, a galaxy may use up all its raw material, ending star birth.

RED AND DEAD

Young, massive stars shine with a bluish light, but they do not live for long before exploding as **supernovae.** When star formation ends, older and cooler stars begin to dominate a galaxy. These stars shine with a reddish light. As a result, the light from aging galaxies appears to come from the red end of the **spectrum.**

With the passage of many billions of years, most of the stars in a galaxy will become white dwarfs and other dim bodies. At the end of its life, a galaxy will shine only in its core, where the last clouds of dust and gas may form some new stars. When its last star dies, a galaxy will go dark.

After a star uses up all its fuel, it stops glowing and becomes a black dwarf, a dark cinder adrift in space.

Galaxies grow dim as their stars age and they use up all of their dust and gas.

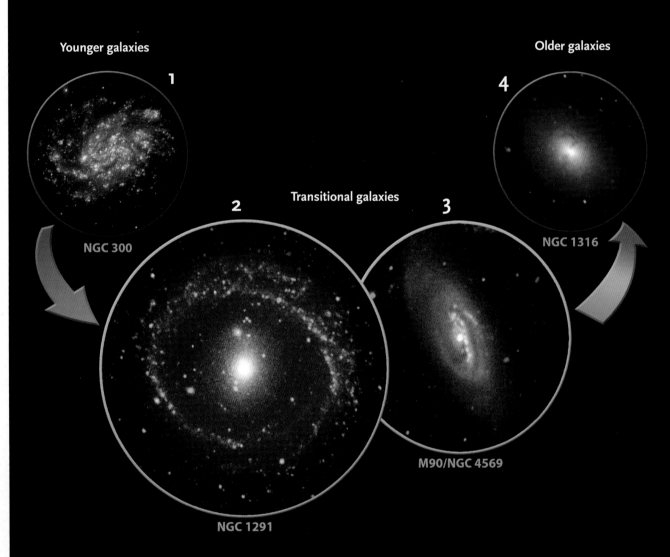

EVOLUTION OF A GALAXY

Younger galaxies

Older galaxies

1

4

NGC 300

NGC 1316

Transitional galaxies

2

3

NGC 1291

M90/NGC 4569

Galaxies pass through various stages of development. NGC 300 (1) is a young galaxy, bright with star birth. A smaller galaxy may have passed through the core of NGC 1291 (2), creating a ring structure. The galaxy M90 (3) has been stripped of gas, greatly reducing star formation. The galaxy NGC 1316 (4) is becoming an elliptical after repeated collisions. It has little remaining gas.

WHICH CAME FIRST?

Did **stars** or **galaxies** form first? In coming years, astronomers hope to use new, more-powerful telescopes to observe light from the first stars and galaxies to form in the universe. These observations should revolutionize our understanding of how galaxies formed.

Another mystery astronomers continue to explore is whether **black holes** or galaxies formed first. Astronomers now believe that a supermassive black hole can be found in the center of nearly all galaxies. These black holes have so much **mass** (amount of matter) that they could not have formed directly from dying stars. Instead, they may have formed when many smaller black holes merged, early in the formation of galaxies. However, some astronomers believe that the black holes may have formed directly from collapsing **dark matter.** Again, more-powerful telescopes may enable astronomers to solve this mystery.

The Swiss astrophysicist Fritz Zwicky first argued for the existence of dark matter in 1933. Zwicky was studying a cluster of galaxies called the Coma Cluster. The galaxies moved around another too quickly to be held together by the gravitation of their visible matter alone. Zwicky inferred that additional gravitation from dark matter was holding the cluster together.

The collision of four massive galaxy clusters is captured in a composite image made by the orbiting Hubble and Chandra X-ray observatories. Scientists still have much to learn about how galaxies form.

GALAXIES AND DARK MATTER

Astronomers believe that dark matter played a vital role in galaxy formation. Unfortunately, scientists do not yet know what dark matter actually is. They believe dark matter is made up of a kind of particle that has not yet been identified. When scientists solve the riddle of dark matter, they will learn a great deal about the nature of both galaxies and the universe.

Radiation blasts from a supermassive black hole at the center of an elliptical galaxy in an artist's illustration. Once a black hole reaches a certain size, it may cut off star formation in a galaxy by heating and pushing away the gas needed to make new stars.

GLOSSARY

Barred spiral galaxy – A spiral galaxy with a long bulge of material called a bar at its core. Spiral arms typically trail away from the bar.

Big bang – The cosmic explosion that scientists believe began the expansion of the universe.

Black hole – The collapsed core of a massive star. The gravity of a black hole is so strong that not even light can escape.

Blueshift – A shift in light's wavelength toward shorter, blue wavelengths. Light from stars or other bodies approaching the Earth may show blueshift.

Chemical element – Any substance that contains only one kind of atom. Hydrogen and helium are both chemical elements.

Cluster – A concentration of hundreds to thousands of galaxies held together by gravity.

Core – The dense, hot center of a star.

Cosmic microwave background (CMB) radiation – The most ancient electromagnetic radiation in the universe. Variations in the CMB radiation correspond to the distribution of galaxies in the universe today.

Dark matter – A mysterious form of matter that does not reflect or absorb light. The majority of matter in the universe is dark matter.

Doppler effect – The change in wavelength of light or sound caused by the relative motion of the source and the observer.

Dwarf galaxy – A small galaxy, containing only several billion stars.

Electromagnetic radiation – Any form of light, ranging from radio waves, to microwaves, to infrared light, to visible light, to ultraviolet light, to X rays, to gamma rays.

Elliptical galaxy – A galaxy with a shape that somewhat resembles a flattened globe.

Galactic void – A large area that contains no galaxies. Such areas may reach 1 billion light-years across or more.

Galactic wall – A vast structure containing millions of galaxies and stretching across hundreds of millions of light-years.

Galaxy – A vast system of stars, gas, dust, and other matter held together in space by mutual gravitational attraction.

Galaxy group – A concentration of dozens of galaxies held together by gravity.

Gravitational lensing – An effect whereby the gravitational field of extremely massive bodies bends space, acting as a lens that magnifies objects in the distance.

Gravity – The force of attraction that acts between all objects because of their mass.

Helium – The second simplest chemical element. Helium is produced through the nuclear fusion of hydrogen.

Hubble constant – The rate at which the universe is expanding. The Hubble constant is approximately 70 kilometers per second per megaparsec.

Hydrogen – The simplest chemical element. Hydrogen is the most abundant substance in the universe. It fuels most stars.

Infrared light – A form of light with long wavelengths. Also called heat radiation. Infrared is invisible to the unaided eye.

Interstellar medium – The dust and gas between stars in a galaxy.

Irregular galaxy — A galaxy with a patchy, disorderly appearance.

Light-year — The distance light travels in a vacuum in one year. One light-year is equal to 5.88 trillion miles (9.46 trillion kilometers).

Mass — The amount of matter in an object.

Megaparsec — A unit of distance used to measure extremely long distances. It is equal to 1 million parsecs or about 3.26 million light-years.

Microwaves — A kind of radio waves with relatively short wavelengths. Microwaves are invisible to the unaided eye.

Nebula — A cloud of dust and gas in space.

Nuclear fusion — The combination of two or more atomic *nuclei* (cores) to form the nucleus of a heavier element. Nuclear fusion releases the energy that powers stars.

Optical — Of or relating to visible light.

Parsec — A unit of distance used to measure extremely long distances. A parsec equals 3.26 light-years.

Plasma — A gas-like form of matter composed of electrically charged particles.

Quasar — An extremely bright object at the center of some distant galaxies. Scientists believe quasars are powered by supermassive black holes.

Radio waves — The form of light with the longest wavelengths. Radio waves are invisible to the unaided eye.

Redshift — A shift in light's wavelength toward longer, redder wavelengths. Doppler redshift is caused by the Doppler effect. Cosmological redshift is caused by the expansion of the universe.

Satellite galaxy — A relatively small galaxy that orbits around a larger galaxy.

Solar system — The planetary system that includes the sun and Earth.

Spectrum, spectra — Light divided into its different wavelengths. A spectrum may provide astronomers with information about a heavenly body's chemical composition, motion, and distance.

Spiral galaxy — A galaxy with a thin, disk-like structure and sweeping arms of stars wrapped about the galaxy's center.

Star — A huge, shining ball in space that produces a tremendous amount of visible light and other forms of energy.

Supercluster — A giant collection of galaxy groups and clusters containing tens of thousands of galaxies.

Supernova, supernovae — An exploding star that can become billions of times as bright as the sun before gradually fading from view. A supernova occurs when a massive star uses up all its fuel.

Visible light — The form of light human beings can see with their eyes.

Wavelength — The distance between successive crests, or peaks, of a wave. Wavelength is used to distinguish among different forms of light. Radio waves have the longest wavelengths, and gamma rays have the shortest wavelengths.

White dwarf — A star that has exhausted its fuel. A typical white dwarf has about 60 percent as much mass as the sun, but is no larger than Earth.

FOR MORE INFORMATION

WEB SITES

The Cosmic Distance Scale

http://heasarc.gsfc.nasa.gov/docs/cosmic

Zoom out from Earth to the planets and stars, distant galaxies, and beyond to understand how vast our universe is.

First Galaxies

http://www.firstgalaxies.org

Learn what we know so far, and what astronomers may yet discover, about how the universe began and galaxies formed.

HubbleSite Gallery

http://www.hubblesite.org/gallery

The "Picture Album" and "Movie Theater" links display the Hubble's images and videos of galaxies.

The Messier Catalog

http://seds.lpl.arizona.edu/messier/

The "Look at Galaxies" link is a catalog of photographs and descriptions of various types of galaxies.

BOOKS

Astronomy: Every Galaxy Has a Black Hole
by Bryson Gore (Franklin Watts, 2005)

Death Stars, Weird Galaxies, and a Quasar-Spangled Universe
by Karen Taschek (University of New Mexico Press, 2006)

Galaxies: Immense Star Islands
by David Jefferis (Crabtree Publishing, 2009)

Planets, Stars, and Galaxies: A Visual Encyclopedia of Our Universe
by David A. Aguilar (National Geographic Society, 2007)

INDEX

Andromeda Galaxy, 20, 28-29; as galaxy, 38; merger with, 34; satellites of, 30; speed of, 32
asteroids, 55

big bang, 25, 31, 32, 38, 46, 48
black holes, 35, 41, 52-53, 58, 59
blueshift, 43

clusters, 20-21, 58; Abell 1689, 24; CL0024+17, 55; motions in, 30; Virgo, 20
cosmic microwave background (CMB) radiation, 32, 46, 47

dark ages, 46
dark matter, 21, 48, 49, 54, 58, 59
Doppler shift, 42-43

electromagnetic radiation, 8, 40
elements, chemical, 6, 42-43
elliptical galaxies, 6, 10-11, 20; defined, 14-15; formation of, 34, 50-52; orbits of, 30; size of, 22

galactic voids, 20
galactic walls, 20, 48
galaxies, 4-5; death of, 56-57, 59; defined, 6-7; discovery of, 38-39; distance of, 24-25; dwarf, 22, 28, 42, 50; glowing by, 40-41; groups of, 20-21, 30; how they formed, 48-49; light in studying, 42-43; merging and collisions between, 18-19, 34-37, 51-53, 58; nearest, 28-29; number of, 8-9, 44-45; orbits of, 30-31; peculiar, 18-19; presently forming, 52-53; remaining mysteries of, 58-59; satellite, 30; size of, 22-23; speed of, 32-33; starburst, 16; star formation in, 50-51; types of, 9-11; when they formed, 46-47, 58. See also clusters; elliptical galaxies; irregular galaxies; spiral galaxies
galaxies, names of: 3C305, 41; AM 0644-741, 19; Antennae, 36-37; Bird, 36; Black Eye (M64), 7; C153, 50; Canis Major Dwarf, 28; Cartwheel, 18-19; Cigar (M82), 16; IC 1101, 22; IC 2163, 37; I Zwicky 18, 53; M74, 4-5;

M87, 22; M90, 57; Mice, The, 34; NGC 300, 57; NGC 1097, 12; NGC 1132, 15; NGC 1291, 57; NGC 1316, 14, 57; NGC 1569, 17; NGC 2207, 37; NGC 3256, 35; NGC 5866, 4-5; PKS 1127-145, 52; Sagittarius Dwarf Irregular, 23; Sombrero, 13; Stephan's Quintet, 37; Tadpole, 19; Whirlpool, 13. See also Andromeda Galaxy; Milky Way Galaxy
gravitational lensing, 54
gravity, 6, 30, 54-56; and galaxy shape, 34; in galaxy formation, 12, 50; in star formation, 40
Great Attractor, 33
Great Wall, 20

halos, 49
helium, 6, 40, 41
Hubble, Edwin P., 11, 38-39
Hubble constant, 32-33, 38
Hubble Space Telescope, 15, 17, 18, 25, 39, 44
Hubble tuning fork, 10-11
Hubble Ultra Deep Field, 44-45
hydrogen, 6, 40, 41, 46, 48

infrared light, 8, 18, 25, 40
interstellar medium, 6, 12
irregular galaxies, 6, 10-11; defined, 16-17; formation of, 50; Local Group, 20; shape changes of, 34

Keck Observatory, 46

light: in studying galaxies, 42-43; speed of, 25; visible, 8, 12, 18, 25, 40, 44
light-years, 20, 25, 52
Local Group, 20-21, 30-33
Local or Virgo supercluster, 20, 30, 32

Magellanic Clouds, 20, 42, 50, 56
megaparsecs, 32
Milky Way Galaxy, 4, 26-27; Andromeda Galaxy and, 28; as galaxy, 38; in Local Group, 20; mergers with, 34; satellites of, 30-31; size of, 22; speed of, 32-33; star formation in, 50-51
Mt. Wilson Observatory, 38-39

nebulae, 6, 12, 38, 40, 48
nuclear fusion, 40, 41

orbits, 30-31

planets, 55
plasma, 6, 40

quasars, 52-53

radio waves, 8, 25, 41
redshift, 25, 30, 33, 42-43

Skymapper Telescope, 45
Sloan Digital Sky Survey, 44
solar system, 32, 56
space, nature of, 54
spectra, 42-43, 56
spiral galaxies, 6, 10-11; barred, 11, 12; defined, 12-13; formation of, 49; Local Group, 20; merging of, 34-37, 52; nearest, 28-29; orbits of, 30. See also Milky Way Galaxy
stars, 6, 38; death of, 56; dwarf, 56; energy from, 40; formation of, 15, 46, 50-51, 58; light in studying, 42-43; spiral galaxy, 12; stripped-away, 34
sun, 20, 26, 28, 56
superclusters, 20-21, 48; Abell 901/902, 21; motions of, 30. See also Local or Virgo supercluster
supernovae, 40, 42, 56

telescopes, 8, 38-39, 46, 58
Two-Micron Sky Survey, 8

ultraviolet light, 18, 40
universe: birth of, 46-47; expansion of, 8, 25, 30-33, 38, 43; observable, 8, 52

wavelength, 8, 25

X rays, 15, 18, 40, 41

Zwicky, Fritz, 58

ACKNOWLEDGMENTS

The publishers acknowledge the following sources for illustrations. Credits read from top to bottom, left to right, on their respective pages. All illustrations, maps, charts, and diagrams were prepared by the staff unless otherwise noted.

Cover: NASA, ESA, and The Hubble Heritage Team (STScI/AURA)-ESA/Hubble Collaboration

1 NASA, ESA, S. Beckwith (STScI), and The Hubble Heritage Team (STScI/AURA)

4-5 NASA, ESA, and The Hubble Heritage Team (STScI/AURA)

6-7 NASA, ESA, and The Hubble Heritage Team (STScI/AURA); NASA and The Hubble Heritage Team (STScI/AURA)

8-9 NASA/JPL/Two Micron All-Sky Survey; NASA/JPL-Caltech

10-11 NASA/JPL-Caltech/K. Gordon, Space Telescope Science Institute/SINGS Team

12-13 European Southern Observatory; NASA and The Hubble Heritage Team (STScI/AURA); NASA, ESA, S. Beckwith (STScI), and The Hubble Heritage Team (STScI/AURA)

14-15 NASA, ESA, and The Hubble Heritage Team (STScI/AURA); NASA, ESA, M. West (ESO, Chile), and CXC/Penn State University/G. Garmire, et al.

16-17 NASA, ESA, and The Hubble Heritage Team (STScI/AURA); NASA, ESA, and The Hubble Heritage Team (STScI/AURA) and A. Aloisi (STScI/ESA)

18-19 NASA/JPL-Caltech/P. Appleton (SSC/Caltech); NASA and The Hubble Heritage Team (STScI/AURA); NASA/H. Ford (JHU), G. Illingworth (UCSC/LO), M. Clampin (STScI), G. Hartig (STScI)/ACS Science Team/ESA

20-21 © Andrew Zachary Colvin; NASA, ESA, C. Heymans (University of British Columbia, Vancouver), M. Gray (University of Nottingham, U.K.), M. Barden (Innsbruck), and the STAGES collaboration

22-23 NASA, ESA, and A. Feild (STScI); NASA/CXC/UCI/ A. Lewis et al. (X-ray), Pal. Obs. DSS (optical); NASA, ESA, and The Hubble Heritage Team (STScI/AURA)

24-25 NASA, ESA, L. Bradley (JHU), R. Bouwens (UCSC), H. Ford (JHU) and G. Illingworth (UCSC)

26-27 NASA; NASA/JPL-Caltech; © Wally Pacholka, AstroPics

28-29 NASA/Nicolas Martin & Rodrigo Ibata, Observatoire de Strasbourg/ULP/2Mass; NASA/JPL/California Institute of Technology

30-31 WORLD BOOK illustration by Matt Carrington; © Mark Garlick, Photo Researchers

32-33 European Southern Observatory; NASA, ESA, and A. Feild (STScI)

34-35 NASA, H. Ford (JHU), G. Illingworth (UCSC/LO), M. Clampin (STScI), G. Hartig (STScI), the ACS Science Team, and ESA; NASA, ESA, The Hubble Heritage Team (STScI/AURA)/ESA/Hubble Collaboration/A. Evans (University of Virginia, Charlottesville/NRAO/Stony Brook University)

36-37 European Southern Observatory; NASA, ESA, and The Hubble Heritage Team (STScI/AURA)-ESA/Hubble Collaboration; NASA/CXC/CfA/E. O'Sullivan (x-ray), Canada-France-Hawaii-Telescope/Coelum (optical); NASA and The Hubble Heritage Team (STScI)

38-39 © Margaret Bourke-White, Time & Life Pictures/Getty Images; © Roger Ressmeyer, Corbis

40-41 NASA/ESA/SOHO; NASA/CXC/CfA/F. Massaro, et al. (X-ray), NASA/STScI/C. P. O'Dea (optical), NSF/VLA/CfA/F. Massaro, et al. (radio); WORLD BOOK illustration by Matt Carrington

42-43 WORLD BOOK illustration by Ernest Norcia; NASA, ESA, CXC, SSC, STSci

44-45 © M. Blanton, SDSS; NASA/ESA/S. Beckwith (STScI) and the HUDF Team; The Australian National University

46-47 NASA/WMAP Science Team

48-49 WORLD BOOK chart by Matt Carrington; NASA, ESA and G. Bacon (STScI); © HowStuffWorks

50-51 NASA/A. Schaller; NASA, ESA, and the Hubble Heritage Team (STScI/AURA) - ESA/Hubble Collaboration; NASA,ESA, M. Robberto (Space Telescope Science Institute/ESA) and the Hubble Space Telescope Orion Treasury Project Team

52-53 NASA, ESA and G. Bacon (Space Telescope Science Institute); NASA/CXC/A. Siemiginowska (CfA)/J. Bechtold (U. Arizona); NASA, ESA, and A. Aloisi (ESA & STScI)

54-55 WORLD BOOK diagram by Precision Graphics; NASA, ESA, and M. J. Jee (Johns Hopkins University); WORLD BOOK illustration by Matt Carrington

56-57 WORLD BOOK illustration by Matt Carrington; NASA/JPL-Caltech/CTIO/Las Campanas/Palomar

58-59 © Bettmann/Corbis; NASA, ESA, CXC, C. Ma, H. Ebeling, and E. Barrett (University of Hawaii/IfA), et al., and STScI; NASA/JPL-Caltech